THE **WAY** OF **ACHIEVERS**

THE WAY OF ACHIEVERS

HOW TO LIVE A SUCCESSFUL LIFE,
GAIN FINANCIAL FREEDOM,
AND CREATE YOUR OWN BUSINESS

MAITHA J. ALSHAMSI

PARTRIDGE

Library of Congress Control Number:		2018964215
ISBN:	Hardcover	978-1-5437-4743-0
	Softcover	978-1-5437-4742-3
	eBook	978-1-5437-4744-7

Print information available on the last page.

To order additional copies of this book, contact
Toll Free 800 101 2657 (Singapore)
Toll Free 1 800 81 7340 (Malaysia)
orders.singapore@partridgepublishing.com

www.partridgepublishing.com/singapore

CONTENTS

DEDICATION

To whoever is seeking to change their lives by being an achiever and creating their own business.

SPECIAL DEDICATION

To my mother, Alya, who always encouraged and motivated me to become better than myself every day. To my sisters, Fatima, Mariam, Athra and Shaikha, you are the world to me and the brightest stars of my life.

ACKNOWLEDGEMENT

I would like to thank my editor, Katie Chambers, who has been prompt and patient, working her magic to retain my voice throughout every paragraph.

INTRODUCTION

BREAK FROM YOUR COMFORT ZONE TO LIVE THE LIFE OF ACHIEVERS

For many decades, people have lost their drive, the motivation to live an exceptional life. I have seen people adopt a mediocre lifestyle, settling for less than they can be, surprisingly even after spending years in school. However, many spend these years in school often only to acquire a job that would ensure they stay in their comfort zone. In many cases, this isn't the job they've dreamed of; it doesn't even pay what they deserve, and they are not living up to their potential. This is the new way of slavery—slaving at your job, living paycheck to paycheck.

Living this life leaves people feeling empty: working hard for a nine-to-five job without knowing or having a clear purpose, not fulfilling their life's mission, and often not even having time to enjoy life with their families.

Sometimes people think they can work hard now, retire when they are sixty-plus, and then enjoy life for the rest of their life with the pension money that they earned. This cycle is repeated for generation after generation.

I have seen people get sick due to work pressure, which creates all kind of health issues and diseases. Sure, they might be making big bucks with a great salary, but this intense focus on work and the pressures associated with it leads to an imbalanced kind of life and lots of health issues.

THE QUESTIONS YOU SHOULD ASK YOURSELF:

- Do you want to wait until you retire to enjoy life?
- Why do you accept living a mediocre lifestyle?
- Why are you afraid to break through your comfort zone and achieve greatness in life?

If you are living in the twenty-first century, you should not accept living a miserable life like that. With the development in technology and the internet, you should look at life from a different perspective; you should start thinking of ways to generate consistent income so you can decide if you would like to continue working or not.

Money shouldn't be the driving force for the way you choose to live. Yes, it is a force that shapes your lifestyle, but it is not the main force. You should work if you want to, not because you have to.

It is your choice; achievers do have choices.

If you want to pursue your career working for someone else or an organisation, you should at least enjoy what you are doing, which is the key to a successful career path. But what would happen if you lost your job and you didn't have any other sources of income to depend on? You need to create an additional pool of income to secure your financial stability. I can show you how to do that.

If you don't enjoy your current career, it is time to make a change and take action. In this book, I will show you the exact techniques that I used so that you can have what you have always wanted, whether it's a new career or a new business where you are your own boss.

These tactics will inspire you to keep moving and achieve your mission, accomplishing more than you have right now and creating businesses and investments on the side while still enjoying your job, whether that's your current one or a new one. And I promise, you can do all this without feeling overwhelmed or spending too much time, allowing you to continue enjoying life with your loved ones.

HAVE THE CHOICE TO CREATE YOUR OWN LIFESTYLE

This is the lifestyle that I have chosen for myself. Although I created multiple streams of income, I am still working in a bank by choice to provide more value to the marketplace, not because I need to work to earn a living. I do it now for inspiration, for leadership experience, and for the opportunity to network with other business-minded people until I decide I want to leave.

Over the lifetime of my banking career, I have changed from one job to another by choice. I have moved to five different careers with highly paid salaries and high positions, all according to my own choice. This is what I believe is the *achievers' way*!

Achievers always do things differently, and they do more than ordinary people. They inspire and impact others as they create the lives they have always wanted and dreamed of.

If you are like me and do not want to waste time, waiting until you over sixty to retire happily, then this book is made exactly for you.

This is a new beginning for you to change this and transform your life into something you never thought possible before this day. Through this book, you will discover the way of achievers.

You Are on a Mission

I am on a mission to have a positive impact in your life and to open your mind to more possibilities. You have a mission to step outside your comfort zone and take charge of your happiness with your career and financial security. I assure you that this book will change your view about many things around you; it is like no other book you have ever read. This book will give you a different perspective and transform your life.

I will not only be your friend in this journey, but I will be your coach as I guide you along your mission to think differently and grow your thinking from where you are to where you want to be in a short period. I will share my personal stories to get you to tap into your inner self and help you start thinking of all your possibilities.

This book will serve as your roadmap to unlocking the achievers' ways, by providing you with the tools to create your own vision, goals, plans, and actions. As I share with you the secrets that led me to be one of the highest paid in my career and one of the top leaders in business, you will discover how I created businesses both online and offline without having to run them on a daily basis. You too can learn how to do this without diverting your time away from living a happy life and spending time with your loved ones. If you replicate these strategies, you will enjoy living life to the fullest as an achiever.

Are You Ready for a Transformation?

Through my coaching, many have transformed their lives.

Lynda M., one of my students from Malaysia, said, "I would like to say that Maitha is very good at explaining the rules and different strategies, and through her coaching, I was able to get quick results through following her key principles and techniques."

Dina K. from London said, "Maitha genuinely cares about other people's success and happiness. I am drawn to her genuine down-to-earth personality; she is an inspiration to me. Her life experiences and achievements are mind-blowing. Maitha always gives helpful advice, and I can't recommend her highly enough."

Although I don't know what stage of life you are in right now, I promise you this book will inspire you to achieve the goals that you always dreamed of.

If you allow me to coach you through these pages, you too can experience a transformation.

You once believed you could do this when you were an innocent child. But over time, your belief was destroyed as you listened to the negative voices in your head, and you accepted a mediocre lifestyle.

Don't be the person who misses out an opportunity by not taking action and taking too long to decide you want. If you read this far, it means only one thing: you are committed to achieving great things in life, and this can be easily achieved only if you take action.

If you are not willing to risk the unusual, you
will have to settle for the ordinary
—Jim Rohn

The Promise

I will challenge you throughout this book, but it will be worth nothing if you just passively read this book without taking action. The inspiration this book provides will be short-lived. However, when *you* take action, follow the exercises that I am going to give you at the end of each chapter, and start creating things, you will achieve great results. We will work together to interrupt the bad thoughts and habits to help you gain a better perspective for yourself.

These might be *bold* promises I am making, but the fact is that I am standing here before you as a real-life example of what many thoughts to be impossible: a young lady living a traditional and restricted kind of life becoming a successful businesswoman.

This book will inspire you to succeed when everyone around you says "You can't" or, even worse than that, when you think, "I can't." Many told me I couldn't, even my own mother, because I wasn't a man. But I believed in myself, and I did it.

You need to *promise* yourself before diving into this journey with me to set a new standard for yourself, to create a plan with some situational goals as you move ahead, and to *step up*!

Promise yourself that you will lead, not follow. You will *believe*, and you will ignore all self-doubt and negative thoughts that tell you this is not possible for you, as I once thought. If I could change my life to be extraordinary, so can you.

I wish you all the success in the near future, so let's dive into this journey of achievers together.

CHILDLIKE BELIEFS

SECTION 1: HAVING CHILDLIKE BELIEFS TO TEAR DOWN LIMITS TO YOUR VISION

As children, we are often asked by adults, "What do you want to be when you grow up?" In my opinion, the adults who are asking the question have missed the opportunity to be or do what they always dreamed when they were a child. By asking the question, the adult is expressing a wish that they could go back in time to be or do what they once visualised for themselves.

When I was a child, many adults asked me this question in my community, in school, at family gatherings, and wherever. As a dreamer in my early childhood, my answer was, "I want to be an astronaut; I want to discover the space and the stars." You could hear loud laughs straight away after hearing my reply. In school, when teachers asked this question, many children answered that they wanted to be a doctor, a teacher, an engineer, a lawyer, a policeman, a nurse—all these answered were acceptable and ordinary. But when they heard my answer, they thought that I was "extra naughty", and they answered back, "No, you can't." In the United Arab Emirates, there was no space station yet where I could go and learn to be an astronaut (the space station was founded in 2015). It didn't matter that I was good at math and physics, that I was exceptional at solving difficult equations at school that other kids could not solve.

I could be an astronaut. But, my main reason for giving that answer was not that I desperately wanted to be an astronaut. Rather, there was a deeper reason: I didn't want to be ordinary and compared to any of my peers. As a child, I thought differently than the other children did, and I wanted to be different. I wanted to have an exceptional life when I grew up, full of giving and enjoyment. I wanted to be an original and unique thinker and creator. I wanted people to see me as I saw myself: a person who would do great things in life. I wanted to share my vision and leave a legacy.

This is true for you too: each of us is an extraordinary and unique human being who can attract all good things in life.

Go back to your childlike beliefs. Your dream job as a child may not be what you really want today, but tap into that time when you believed you could do and be anything.

I used to watch my father drive his car. I imagined myself driving like him, making those turns, remaining as calm as he did. When I went for my first driving lesson, the instructor asked me if I had ever driven before, and I told her it was my first time. When I started driving with her, she looked at me and said, "You are lying to me. You look like you have driven before." When I told her I was being honest, she asked me to tell me her secrets. I told her I had watched my father drive for many years, visualising the way that I would one day drive.

This shows how important it is to believe and visualise your success.

You need to tap back into that childlike mind, where you find it easy to believe and visualise.

SECTION 2: CAN PARENTS INSTIL OR DESTROY A CHILD'S BELIEFS?

My father had many jobs: a freelance small truck driver carrying soft sands from the desert, a desert tour driver carrying foreigners coming to UAE to see the deserts between the 1960s (before UAE Union) and 1990s, and an investor in a small grocery store with my uncle. With his busy schedule, he always found time for his wife and children. When he took us out every evening, my mother and sisters would go shopping for school requirements and home groceries. Most of the time, I liked to stay with him in the car listening to BBC News on the radio.

One day, while we were listening, I heard a sound of a clock bell chime loudly before the news began. I asked, "Dad, what is this sound?"

He replied with a smile on his face, "That is the sound of Big Ben, the biggest clock tower in the world."

I replied, "But Dad, where is this Big Ben?"

He said, "It is in London, in the United Kingdom."

I replied, "One day I will go there."

My dad replied with a smile again, "Yes, you will. I have no doubt about it." With his simple and short reply, he instilled the belief that a five-year-old child can achieve this goal. At that time, I didn't know how or when this could happen, but I knew that I would get there one day. My dad instilled the belief that I could do whatever I wanted if I was determined, and that strengthened my belief that I was extraordinary, and I would achieve big things in my life.

My dream did become a reality. With eight children in my family, I am the only one who travelled to London (which ended up being my main business hub) as well as many other places in the world.

The point that I want to make here is that even if you don't know how and when you will achieve a goal, whether small or big, you must instil that belief in your inner self that you can do it. Without believing it, you can't sustain your life's goals. And if you are a parent, you have the responsibility to instil that belief in your child.

My father was an achiever himself. At the age of four, he became an orphan with no one except my uncle who was two years older than him. When my father was 14 years old, he went to Bahrain to work. (This was before the discovery of petrol in my country, so the entire region was poor). He went to work and learned many skills, then moved to Saudi Arabia to work and build his own fortune with my uncle. When he turned 24, he built a house and married my mother. His life was full of achievements: he invested his money in real estate and built a small business with my uncle and never worked for somebody else.

Unfortunately, my dad died in October 1998, when I was 21 years old, after suffering from a brain tumour for five years. He got this disease when I was just about to graduate from high school, which caused a major shift in my life. I was no longer my father's special little daughter, growing under his guidance; instead, I had to face life on my own with all its challenges. After he passed, I felt the pressure to create a desirable life for myself and be in control of my decisions as soon as possible.

I could do this because my father has raised me that way. He understood the life of achievers, and he instilled that in me. He taught me how to fix wires at homes like an electrical engineer, as well as television systems, electrical cables, and lamps. While most fathers in my country would never teach these things to a girl, my father knew I could do it and that I could make my own decisions in many areas of life, including creating my own businesses.

yes, a parent can instil or destroy a child's beliefs. If your parent destroyed yours, get them back, and if you have children, make sure you set them up for a lifetime of achievement.

If you have children, let them dream, let them have a childhood vision for themselves. You should not restrict their vision. Tell them that they can be whatever they want to be. Do not superimpose your dreams for them. We so often hear of the mother telling her child to be a doctor when he or she grows up because that was the mother's dream that she did not accomplish. When that happens, the child may grow up having a miserable life, living someone else's dream. You need to encourage them to enlarge their vision and support them all the way to realise their purpose and achieve their goals in life. This is exactly what my dad did for me when I was a kid— always encouraging, always supporting, and always listening to me tell my stories about what I wanted to become.

CHAPTER SUMMARY:

- Go back to your childlike beliefs to get rid of any limitations on your vision.
- If you're a parent, encourage your children in their childlike beliefs.
- Know your purpose and fulfil your dreams in life.

THE MAIN SECRET TO ALL ACHIEVERS' SUCCESS

2

In this chapter, you will learn the importance of having a strong vision and learn the step-by-step process to creating your own vision.

While reading through this chapter, I want you to think about these questions:

- What would you like to create or be in the next six to twelve months?
- If you were to stop thinking about the past, whether it is past failures or procrastination, what new vision would you create for yourself right now?

It is not about your destination. It is about your journey— your vision.

SECTION 1: WHAT IS A VISION?

A vision is nothing more than having the design and creative image of your dreams to turn them into reality.
—Maitha Al Shamsi

A vision is an image or picture that you create in your mind about yourself and your own success. It is nothing more than the design and thinking of how you want your immediate future to look. A vision is a collection or combination of goals which create a true picture of what you want to be or whom you want to become. A true vision is what you see yourself having or doing in the future. You could write a vision for your life in three years, five years, or ten years. This is your roadmap, so when you have a clear purpose, you will have a clear vision.

When creating a vision, write it down on paper in all its specific detail. Begin with your purpose—why you want it—and then imagine what your life would look like if you achieved that vision. Specify every detail of your vision in your journal and have a short version you can think about every day. Just like that childlike belief, feel it as if were real. This will instil a belief in your vision, which will allow your subconscious mind to work towards achieving that ultimate vision. When you have a vision, you are basically giving a map to your subconscious mind to calculate the possibilities to achieve it so that every day it will take you one step forward to your ultimate goals.

If after some time you realized this is not the vision you wanted, that's okay; you just need to recreate a new one and start working towards it again. As dynamic human beings, we tend to change our thoughts and views over time as we grow. And so our vision changes along with it. Sometimes, your vision stays the same but you need to change the details. You may need to change the action steps needed to reach the goals as you grow because you get a clearer direction of where you are heading.

Regardless of whether it changesor not, it is always important to have a clear vision. Without having a clear vision, you don't know where you are heading. Of course, you will end up somewhere, but do you want to settle for just any place? Imagine this: You are driving a car, and you want to go somewhere, but you don't know exactly where you want to be. You will just drive aimlessly and see where it takes you. But if you know exactly where you want to be (the end goal), then you will start driving towards that destination. It is exactly the same with visions.

SECTION 2: REASONS TO CREATE A VISION

Here are the top three reasons why you should create your own unique, crystal-clear vision.

1. The vision will always move you forward, like a map

Having a vision, whether big or small, will set up a milestone for more growth in your life, and you will know exactly where you want to go and work towards it. Relatively, it is difficult to accomplish anything without knowing your real vision. Having a clear vision will provide shortcuts; it will create opportunities even without you knowing about it, as thinking about your vision will send vibrations into the universe to help you reach what you want. It will provide you with confidence and persistence towards working and achieving goals in the short term.

Start writing your first three-year vision, five-year vision, and ten-year vision.

I remember when I wrote my first vision. I was 21 years old. I had written it clearly, stating I wanted to be financially free before I reached 35, and I wanted my mother to observe my success and enjoy it with me. At that time, I didn't know how I was going to achieve it, as I was in very deep debt. But I had that strong belief that if I continued finding ways to create an extra income, I wouldn't have to worry about my next paycheck. It took me a while until I realised that vision. I moved jobs and then built a couple of businesses to achieve my ultimate picture.

So start working on your vision now, and make it crystal clear, and you will have the reason to jump out of your bed every morning, moving you forward.

2. By having a vision, you will lay the groundwork so you always have something to go back to

If you have a vision, you will always have it to go back to when mistakes arise, and your life takes a wrong turn.

Sometimes, you may take steps towards your vision, and for whatever reason it doesn't work out. Having these kinds of circumstances is fine. We all are learning. I previously took some steps to establish a business with two other people who came to me and wanted to be my partners, but after a while, it didn't work out, which made me realise that although I was taking this direction, it was not necessarily the right one towards my vision.

As with anything you do, you either succeed or you learn and grow. There is no failure in the world of achievers; it is always about learning new things in the spirit of curiosity. In my case, I had to learn why this business failed so I could apply it to future business endeavours. I realised I didn't have the right partners, ones who matched my expectations when it came to running this kind of business. The two partners were depending on me to fund and run the business so they could share the profits of the business at the end of every month and year. Therefore, I was the one who decided not to continue this business, despite small losses that I incurred when registering the company, and I moved on by going back and reviewing my vision and continuing with my craft.

I learned this again from my coach when someone came to me and wanted to establish a unique options trading brokerage company in Dubai. My coach asked me questions to help me decide whether I should do it. When my coach asked me, "What do you think is the main reason this person wants to establish this business with you? Why doesn't he do it himself?"

Upon reflection, I realized this person wanted to be my partner to give him citizenship in my country, and he needed me to invest and quit my current work while he kept travelling to the United States and other countries, teaching people how to trade.

My coach then asked me if this decision resonated with my ultimate vision. It was clearly diverting me from my vision, so I decided not to move forward.

By continually revisiting my vision, I ensured I made the right decisions and was on the right path. Therefore, by creating a vision, you too can use it to steer you in the right direction. This vision lays the groundwork for success.

By the way, I suggest you have a coach in all areas of your life. The coach will help you achieve your vision and goals in a shorter time than you expected and will hold you accountable to help you build the needed discipline and achieve it.

The more details you put into your vision, the better groundwork you build for yourself. For me, the details included what kind of business I wanted to have, what characteristics I wanted in a partner, where I wanted my business to be located, and other things to make my business successful.

When you read your vision every day, you can go back to it and make it clearer, which will help you get closer to what you want. These steps are very important when you follow this routine every day and take actions.

Because I had a clear vision of what I wanted, when a new business opportunity was presented to me, I knew what decision to make, whether this business would serve my purposes or not.

I always ask myself the following two most powerful questions when something comes into my way.

1. Does this align with my vision?
2. Is this a part of my mission?

If you want a better life full of purpose that will lead you to your vision, then you must ask yourself these questions. These are simple questions, but believe me, they are very powerful. They will cause you to think about what you are going to do next and keep you on track of your overall vision.

3. The vision will not only inspire you but will help you inspire others

When you are working towards your vision, it will reveal the real you—the way you act and network, the original creative ideas you can create—and this will inspire others. People will be attracted to you because you have a vision and you are working hard to reach it.

People will be hungry to learn from you and be guided by you. That is no surprise at all. People of the right mindset will be attracted to you like a magnet.

Achievers are successful in all areas of their lives. As they work towards achieving great things, they will have great relationships.

Section 3: The Process to Create a Clear Vision

As I mentioned above, the first step to creating a vision is having a clear purpose, the reason why you want that ultimate vision for yourself.

Ask yourself, "Why am I here on Earth?" You are unique; there is no one like you among the entire 7.2 billion people living on this Earth. You are here for a purpose, and you have things to accomplish, so don't let this chance pass you by. Grab the opportunity in front of your eyes. Stop procrastinating and stop blaming situations or the economy.

I love this quote from Jim Rohn, given in one of his lectures: *"Success is something you attract by the person you become. For things to improve, you have to improve. For things to get better, you have to get better. For things to change, you have to change. When you change, everything will change for you."*

So start to improve now by following these steps to create your vision:

1. Decide what you want in each area of your life and why it is important for you to achieve it.
2. Write your vision.
3. Now draw out your vision. Initially, I learned that the vision should be created from pictures cut from magazines or newspapers showing how you want your life to look, such as your dream house, car, business, travels, etc. But then I learned from attending a very powerful seminar called "Mission to Millions", a signature program of T. Harv Eker, that you need to draw your vision. The vision will have greater meaning when it's drawn, not when you cut and paste pictures from somewhere else into your board. Even if you are

the worst artist, as I am, the vision will have deeper meaning for you when it's drawn.

4. Think about the beliefs and habits you need to develop to support you on your process of creating this vision.

5. Determine what you need to acquire along the way: Is there a skill you need to learn, a new career that you want to have, a new business you want to establish, a new way you want to adopt?

6. Create a mastermind group to support you in the process. A mastermind group is a group of people who share the same vision as you and have achieved what you want. They can share their experiences with you and support you along the way.

7. Show gratitude and thank the Creator for what you have. This is an important element to success, as it sends good vibrations into the universe and helps you receive more good things.

8. Plan a course of action (small goals) to follow each day to achieve this vision. (The next chapter will teach you how to do this.)

9. Always believe that this is meant for you and not anybody else.

SECTION 4: TOOLS TO HELP YOU ACHIEVE YOUR VISION

As you see, having a vision can help you become clear on what you want to become, where you want to go, and what you want to accomplish. However, sometimes it is hard to make your vision a reality when you are facing lots of challenges. There are four tools you can use to help it come to fruition.

1. Define your mission to instil more motivation

It is difficult to sustain motivation over a long period—and even more difficult if you don't have the right mindset or the right people around you. If you are not in an environment that encourages you to continue, you may stop believing in yourself or achieving your vision. But once you have a personalised mission, it will direct you towards what you want to achieve in the near future.

Many achievers create a mission, the secret ingredient to achieving their vision. Your mission is your inner world, or inner self, that guides you towards your vision (which is your outer world). It might sound ridiculous at first, but this is the reality of every person who achieved success: they were always on a mission. It is not enough to just say you are on a mission. Much like writing and drawing out your vision, you need to write your mission statement to keep you motivated and inspired to do whatever it takes to fulfil that mission.

For example, my mission statement is to inspire and encourage others to find the way of achievers, living a life full of abundance and fulfilment.

Even if you are in the dark side of your life, keep reminding yourself daily of your mission and purpose in life.

2. Use your imagination to help sustain your vision

Imagination is part of the process that leads us to a bigger vision in our lives. The imagination of your vision shows you what the end result will look like and motivates you to get there in a short time.

The vision is the broader picture, while imagination is a process you do on a daily, weekly, and monthly basis to strengthen that vision and keep it alive and envision the end results.

Imagination is a powerful tool, and I suggest that you use it for positive things, because it works either way. But guess what: it is ten times more powerful if you use it for good things.

You see, all invention and creation in the world first started with an imagination. My country, the United Arab Emirates, which is only 42 years old as I write this book, was a vision created by the founder, Sheikh Zayed Bin Sultan Al Nahyan, who created a masterpiece from pure desert land when everyone around him said that it was not possible. However, he did not listen, and he kept working based on his heart to fulfil his inner mission to form this country into one of the leading economic, industrial, and tourist countries in the world.

People from all over the world come to UAE to work, do business, invest, and create a decent and secure living for their families. For more than forty-seven years, this country is a safe haven for many people around the world who are looking for peaceful and secure lives. The tallest building in the world, Burj Khalifa; the Palm Islands of Dubai; the biggest mall in the world, Dubai Mall; and the recent Dubai Water Canal were created by the imagination and vision of Sheikh Mohammed Bin Rashid Al Maktoum, and his late father, Sheikh Rashid Bin Saeed Al Maktoum.

On the technology side, Apple, Microsoft, Facebook, and the internet were all first created in the human mind by the power of imagination. We would not be enjoying all these now if it weren't for imagination. We could be still in the dark if Edison hadn't invented the light bulb.

My life was a great force of imagination. I created the environment that I wanted even when I was in my worst situations. I imagined my peace of mind, the jobs that I wanted, where I wanted to be in every cycle of my life, all by the power of my imagination.

I am not saying that you should just imagine and not get to work. Imagination works only when you put it into action. Dreaming is one thing and imagining and working towards what you have envisioned, with strong belief, is something else entirely. Darren Hardy, the publisher and CEO of *Success* magazine, mentioned how he met his wife. He first created a vision that indicated he would be married. That is the first step: identify what you want in your vision, as we discussed how to do in the last section. Then he created an image in his mind about his future wife (i.e., he used his imagination). To act on that, he wrote a full description of what he envisioned his future wife would be like, complete with details, specifying even the small things, like how she dealt with him, how she would raise their children, and so on, and then he imagined himself in a position of deserving this woman. He then went to work on making himself attractive to this type of woman. Two years later, he met with this woman he had envisioned, and she ended up becoming his loving soul mate.

3. Keep your end goal in mind

Since my vision was to be debt-free. I knew that my end goal was money. Therefore, I didn't let other things distract me—like staying in jobs I enjoyed but that didn't pay what I needed.

When I started my career as a banker, I was a clerk in the clearing department, posting cheques all day long. During the first six months of joining the bank, I did rotation training on all the bank's departments, such as treasury, credit, corporate, trade, transaction banking, customer service, clearing, and HR. From that time, I had a target in mind: I wanted to work in the corporate department because of the experience that I would gain by learning about corporate companies in various industries. I had this in mind for three years.

I was still working in the clearing department and completing my study in college in the evening. For these three years, I looked for any opportunity to get into corporate, but my qualifications did not match their requirements.

However, I didn't give up that dream of becoming a corporate banker. Sometimes things do not happen instantly. However, just keep the end in mind.

One evening when I completed my work in the clearing department, I was about to leave work, and I saw the cash department team still working. They were overloaded.

When I saw them in this situation still working late, even though I needed to go home and study, I went directly in and offered my support while all my colleagues in the clearing departments left for home. During my work with them, the manager in charge of the branch saw that I was working with them. She asked me if I wanted to move to this department permanently. I didn't, but I realized this was the opportunity I had been waiting for three years, so I told her, "If you want to move me somewhere, I would like to be moved to the corporate department."

The manager in charge was really surprised with my answer, since corporate is one of the toughest departments, requiring special skills and qualifications. When she told me I didn't have the needed skills, I replied, "I can learn. Nothing is impossible. I know I can." She granted my request, with one condition: I had to train with the corporate team. After a month, they would write a report on my performance, and she would then decide if I could stay at corporate.

For one month, I sacrificed my time after work. I skipped lunch every day and worked extra hours in corporate before heading to class. At the end of the month, I was qualified, and the manager in charge signed my transfer papers to be transferred to the corporate department as a relationship officer. For the four years I worked there, I learned and gained good experiences.

After that, I continued changing jobs as soon as I gained the needed experience, moving on to a new job to learn new skills.

Jim Rohn said, *"We get paid for bringing value to the marketplace. It takes time, but we get paid for the value, not the time."*

Therefore, the more you bring value to the marketplace, the more you get paid. The more value you provide, the more you get paid in any market and in any industry. Thus, by keeping my end goal in mind, I focused on learning more skills so I could get paid more money.

4. Establish a Good Morning Routine

I have created a daily routine which helped me sustain my progress and motivated me when I was on the downside or felt like I did not want to do anything. Good daily routines can help you achieve your vision.

I also discovered that ultra-successful people, the achievers, use these morning routines to remind themselves of who they are and what they want to achieve.

Let me share with you my morning routine, which I learned from my coaches, mentors, and the most successful people I know.

- I wake up at 5 a.m.
- I start with a prayer to Almighty God, Allah, my Creator.
- I meditate for twenty minutes, focusing on different areas of my life that I selected for each stage. It could be health, my business/career, my wellbeing, or money.

I have used many programs for meditation. The best I have found are the programs of John Assaraf, which have helped me over the last seven years.

- After the meditation, I spend at least five to ten minutes journaling. In the journal, I write:
  - Ten things that I am grateful for.
  - Three to five things I want to accomplish or achieve for that day. These can be small and simple tasks, like going to the gym, playing for one hour, or reading for thirty minutes. Remember, these small goals will accumulate to big things over time. The key here is consistency in everything that you do.

This is my simple morning routine. Most achievers have something similar, or an even more regimented system. Some achievers add in morning exercise, like ten push-ups every morning or a fifteen-minute aerobics routine to boost their energy.

COACHING TIPS:

- Grab a pen and paper and write down what you have learned from this chapter.
- Decide what action you can take right now to meet your vision and change your current reality. This doesn't necessarily have to be a big action: it could be something small like updating your resume, searching about an online business idea, or even planning your first meal to start your diet journey from tomorrow.

COACHING EXERCISE: CREATING A VISION

Take a moment to stop thinking logically and start thinking with your heart. Have a deep feeling. Imagine yourself when you were a child, four to seven years old. Then imagine yourself as an adult. Reflect on all the important moments in your life—your skills, your contribution to your community, your job, etc. Use that reflection to fill out this worksheet.

The purpose of my life is...
(e.g., **to give, to share my experience, to coach others to succeed in their lives by ...**)

What do I want in each area of my life?
(e.g., **relationships—a loving and caring family; career—my own business; spirituality—a stronger relationship with my creator**)

Places I want to travel to and adventures I want to take
(e.g., **to discover ancient Peru, to visit Rome and Japan, to experience parachute jumping, to volunteer with Earth Watch to conserve Koala in Australia**)

Things I would like to learn or do
(e.g., learn a new language, learn photography)

Write down your vision based on the things you listed in the previous three questions, and then draw it out:
(e.g., My ultimate vision is to live a life full of abundance and fulfilment in health, wealth, business, career, and relationships)

To fulfil my vision, I will need to acquire the following beliefs, habits, skills, etc., which will support me during the process.
(e.g., I need to acquire special skills by attending business courses on how to systemize my business online. I need to set up the habit of checking in on my goal progress daily.)

Where can I go and whom can I turn to, to create my mastermind group?
(e.g., search for likeminded people whenever I travel and meet new people who will support my vision and my mission.)

It is important to give back to achieve what you desire. What are you keen to give back in return?

I am going to give back or contribute in the following way:

(e.g., become part of the Earth Watch environmental community, where I will contribute my time and money at least once a year to nature and wildlife; teach, coach, and mentor people on trading in financial markets and on wealth creation)

Now, what is your mission that you live by?

My mission in this life is...

(e.g., to inspire and encourage others to the way of achievers by living a life full of abundance and fulfilment)

Things that I want to create for me through this vision:

(e.g., enjoy life with my mother and the rest of the family, share my wealth with them)

CHAPTER SUMMARY:

- A vision is having the design and creative belief of your dreams to turn them into reality.
- It is important to have a clear vision so your subconscious mind can work towards achieving your goals.
- By creating a vision, you will stop yourself from making bad decisions.
- A vision will give you more clarity and more awareness of what you want to do and how you can get back on track.
- To create a vision, you need to determine your purpose and what you want in each area of your life.
- Once you know what you want, write/draw out your vision.
- Determine the skills, habits, and beliefs you will need to make your vision a reality.
- Create a mission statement, use your imagination, keep the end in mind, and establish good morning routines to help you achieve your vision.

HOW TO ACHIEVE SUCCESS WITH LESS EFFORT

3

To achieve success, you must have a plan. Planning has helped me all the way; in fact, it saved me from staying in debt for a long time. I became an expert in planning as I did it for myself. I always visualise how things will be and then plan how I can get through any problem and solve it in a short period. Over time, it became so systematic that I started planning everything in my life automatically. I will be teaching you planning skills in this chapter.

If you don't design and plan your own life, someone else will have you on their agenda and planning for their own purpose and benefits. This will lead you to neglect yourself and live a life full of resentment. You must not let that happen. Design your own life.

SECTION 1: EFFORTLESS FORMULA

The main key to realising your vision is creating goals and establishing a plan with action steps.

There is a formula to achieve success with less effort, no matter what type of success you seek, health, wealth, financial, business, relationships, etc.

To achieve success, you need to follow this two-part formula. Part one is to get in the right mindset: make sure you are clear about what you want to achieve, create that meaningful goal, and then ask yourself, "What is it going to look like and feel like when I complete it?" Part two is to take it from your mind into action. However, you have to make sure you take the right action steps. So, ask yourself, "What is the exact process I need to apply and practice in order to achieve that goal?" The art is to know what to do, in the right order, and at the right time, then take small steps every day to achieve it.

Many people work too hard because they don't take the time to back off, learn the process, and practice it. It is all about small steps every day rather than trying to bite off more than you can chew or, worse, just going to training course after training course or reading book after book and never even reviewing or applying what you have learned.

Over time, I have learned that "slow is smooth and smooth is fast". Once you take the time to be clear about what you need to do and spend a little bit of time each day, you can achieve amazing things with less time.

STEPS TO ACHIEVING YOUR GOAL IN LESS TIME:

Part 1: Mindset

1. Set up a meaningful goal that keeps you energised to achieve it. Ask yourself, "What will it mean to me if I achieve this goal?" The goal should make you jump out of bed every morning and cause you to stay up at night doing the activities that will move you closer to your goals.

2. Put your goal in writing, in a journal, if you have one. This way, you can refer to it, memorise it, and improve any of the action points as you go along. This will increase the chances that you will achieve your goals because it creates an energy force that gets you into the work to reach that goal.

3. Envision what the goal will look like upon completion.

Part 2: Action

4. Plan it precisely: Write your plan with at least three action steps needed to complete the goal. For each action step, include all the details. For example, if you want to lose weight, you could plan to go to the gym. However, then you need all the details: how often you will go, what you will do while you are there, etc. To plan all the details ask the following:

   a. What are the fundamental skills I need?

   b. What are the details for each strategy/action step?

   c. How can I be clearer? Be clear on what exactly needs to be done to meet this goal. Being clear about what you want is a real power. Clarity is in itself a real power, and power is the motivational force that drives you to take action.

5. Schedule time to work on your action steps a little bit every day.

6. Set a timeline for when you are going to achieve it.

7. Make it difficult to draw back. Ask yourself, "What action can I take in this moment of goal-setting to commit myself, so I do not back out?" At first, it might be too scary because you will be pushing yourself to do something that you haven't done or aren't used to doing, but this will give you the commitment to move on with

your goal. If you want to learn a new skill or be coached by someone who has already achieved that goal, go ahead and pay for the full tuition fees in advance. This will make it more painful if you decide to give up, and it will give you the drive to proceed with what you wanted.

8. Create your own *mastermind alliance*: A mastermind alliance is a group of people with similar visions and goals. Try to find people who are already successful in the area that you want to be in. If you want to be rich, surround yourself with rich people. If you want to be happy, surround yourself with happy people and learn skills from them. Over time, I had learned to stay far away from negative people who discourage my vision and trick me to live below my means. I used to have friends who were stuck for years without making any improvements in their lives until I decided to surround myself with positive and encouraging people who support me and encourage me to move ahead.

In order to get to the state where everything looks effortless (the point where you see a person earning a good income or running a successful business with ease, or playing a music instrument flawlessly without effort), you must put in hard work daily. Once you do, it will be a subconscious, effortless thing to maintain.

SECTION 2: THE POWER OF HAVING A JOURNAL

I remember when I first started writing in a journal. It was not easy at first, but when I realised I was progressing in my way of thinking, I discovered it was worth the time I spent each and every day. You cannot depend entirely on your memory. Journaling is very important to track your progress.

I had a moment when I went through my old journal and discovered that I had achieved five out of the seven goals I had written down with a timeline, although I had achieved them on a greater scale than I envisioned. I now coach my clients to start journaling what they experience each day. Always have a journal to write your goals and your progress; this will help you achieve great growth.

The fact about journaling is that it doesn't have to make sense; you don't need to follow any order to writing. What you write in your journal can be whatever comes enters your mind that day, whatever experiences you have, any new ideas or lessons that you learn, or any situation, good or bad, that you are currently going through. Keeping a journal helps to release the stress and emotions you may be carrying around as you deal with life's situations. Writing clears your mind and releases stress. Once you write it down, leave it on the paper and move on.

If you don't write what you face each day, then you may or may not remember it, but if you keep writing what you are experiencing, the chances are greater you will remember it. You will also not repeat the same mistake again if you write about a bad experience and what you have learned from it. Journaling improves your mental clarity; it grants the ability to see your life in a bigger picture, and it serves as evidence for every success you've had.

In my own journal, I write my monthly goals. At the end of the month, I go back and assess what I haven't yet achieved and compliment myself for what I have. In addition, I go back every year and write a summary of the places I travelled to during the year, the emotions about those places, and the achievements I had when I travelled there. I then write what I have achieved during the year and set goals for the next year.

In short, journals help you track your personal growth and success, provide clarity, help you understand your own emotions, help you solve problems, and improve your overall focus. So start today: have a journal beside your pillow and start journaling your *a-ha* moments.

SECTION 3: SKILLS TO HELP YOU ACHIEVE

Along with taking action by implementing the effortless formula and using the power of writing in your journal, you will want to cultivate some skills that can help you achieve success.

Delegation: I discovered my leadership skills when I was playing with a neighbour's children. I used to plan their weekend, arranging small weekend plays or parties. I gave everyone a role. Thus, at an early age, I discovered my gift and talent in the art of delegation. Delegation is very important for any leader in any business or career role. To be more productive in business or in your career, you must learn this skill. I have seen many managers who do not know how to delegate, and they are stuck doing unnecessary things that do not bring real value. When I think of the art of delegation, I always imagine an orchestra: the leader of the orchestra does not play all the instruments. Everyone has a role to play to create the harmonic music played by the team.

Creativity and imagination: I remember playing imagination games as a child. Each of us had to imagine a story and then tell part of the story every weekend. It was like creating a movie scene. One of my childhood friends ended up working in a local magazine as a reporter. Another became a teacher. They both still use this skill. Even if you don't end up in a job where it is apparent you need this skill, creativity and imagination can help you meet your goals.

Seek after learning: Although I was not the cleverest girl in school and did not score high grades all the time, I always knew what I wanted. I liked to read books to feed my curiosity about the universe and the galaxy. I read the book *A Brief History of Time*, a book about quantum physics by Stephen Hawking, when I was 11 years old. This book made me think about the world around us and how it was formed. Due to my passion and curiosity, I always had something new to learn every day. Chapter 7 will discuss the importance of this skill in more detail.

Persistence: It is an important skill, so I wanted to briefly highlight it here. You have to believe that you will achieve. The secret to this is persistence and believing that you will achieve whatever you desire sooner or later. On the other hand, if you stop, you will end up like the people who are unhappy and unfulfilled in their lives.

COACHING TIPS

Set up weekly and monthly plans

Opportunities arise every day, and if you don't plan properly, you will lose the chance to grab them. However, if you plan and set goals, your life will be full of energy.

Once you have specified your yearly goals on paper, break them into small action steps that can be achieved monthly, weekly, and daily, setting routines and activities.

Remember: Always set new goals as soon as you achieve the first goals.

Coaching Exercise 1: Applying the Effortless Formula

In the last exercise, you listed your vision, the things you want for yourself: upgrading your house, buying a luxury car, learning to speak in public, setting up a new business, teaching your skills to others, taking horse-riding lessons, travelling to new places, etc.

Pick one of those things and walk through the following effortless formula with it.

1. Set up a meaningful goal that will help and motivate you to achieve it.
2. Take a moment to envision what the goal will look like upon completion.
3. Plan at least three actions that you can take right now to achieve this goal within the next twelve months.

Action Step #1: (e.g., go to the gym)

Provide all the details for this action step:

What fundamental skills or tools will you need to complete this action step (e.g., knowledge of exercise equipment, exercise clothes)?

What are the details for this action step (e.g., go to the gym three times a week for one hour, completing a workout for a different muscle group each day)?

Action Step #2: (e.g., eat healthy meals)

Provide all the details for this action step:

What are the fundamental skills or tools you will need to complete this action step?

What are the details for this action step?

Action Step #3: (e.g., create weekly grocery list to buy produce)

Provide all the details for this action step:

What are the fundamental skills or tools you will need to complete this action step?

What are the details for this action step?

1. Create a weekly schedule, carving out time each day to work on these action steps.
2. Determine when you will achieve this goal.
3. What system can you put in place to ensure you will not back out on this goal (e.g., pay for the gym in advance, report to your mastermind group what you ate)?
4. List people who could be a part of your mastermind alliance group or where you could go to find one.

CHAPTER SUMMARY

- You always need to have a plan.
- Prepare for the right mindset by creating a meaningful goal, writing it down, and envisioning your success.
- Plan precisely with full details for all your action steps.
- Schedule time daily to work on your goals and set a deadline.
- Write in your journal to track your progress and provide clarity.
- Cultivate the ability to delegate, imagine, and persist.
- Seek after learning opportunities.

PLANNING FOR FINANCIAL SUCCESS

If you want one year of prosperity, grow seeds; if you want ten years of prosperity, grow trees. If you want a lifetime of prosperity, grow your self-worth.
—Chinese proverb

Section 1: You Can Become Financially Free

Do you want to continue in your career but your job isn't helping you become financially free? Do you not want to worry about your employer laying you off? Do you want to have your own business running for you while you only manage it overall but do not have to be involved in the day-to-day operations? Do you want to have a business but don't want to be overwhelmed with many things you cannot control and live the lifestyle that you have always wanted?

All that can happen if you diversify your income from a standard job into income-generation machines, such as investments or your own business.

When I first decided to change my lifestyle from being solely an employee to creating multiple streams of income from my own businesses and trading, I had to create a plan to become financially free. My plan was to be financially free within six months. However, with all my debts, it took a year and a half. You need to make sure you set realistic plans.

Work on a plan to become financially free within a realistic period. First, create a vision of your business module, then search for the business that you love based on your passions and skills and what you want to be in the near future by creating this business. Then find a way to systemize and leverage or multiply this business module by going online.

ASK YOURSELF:

1. What kind of investment or business do you want to start?
2. Is it based on what I really love, my skills, and my passion?
3. Does it help solve people's problems?
4. Can this business be systemized so that I don't need to be in the business but can monitor it from time to time? (This will be discussed in detail in the following chapter.)
5. Will it positively affect my lifestyle and not add any pressure?

If you answered yes on most of the above questions, then this is the best business you can create. In the next chapter, I will show you how to create your business.

Section 2: Creating the Right Plan with the Right Steps

Now that you have realised you can become financially free, you will need to create a plan following the effortless formula I showed you in the last chapter. However, I want you to know that sometimes you have to revisit your plan because you didn't initially have the right steps. This happened to me.

I had the idea to diversify my income into investments when I was just starting my career. At that time, my sister and I were the first ones from my family to enter into the banking sector. Not a single person from my family or extended family knows about banking, and not many were running their own business while they were still working. I heard that one of my cousins had done this, but he was not willing to share his secrets, as he was secretly managing his business.

My uncles were businessmen. My older uncle had sports stores all over Emirates of Sharjah and investments in properties. My second uncle owned a grocery store he shared with my father and investments in properties, but they were unwilling to share their experience with a little girl like me. I heard from my older brothers that my uncle used to sit with his sons when they were still children every evening to pass on his business experience and involve them in his work. It was a great mindset, and I wish I could have had this experience.

Thus, when I found my passion in trading the global financial market, more specifically, the foreign exchange market, I didn't have anyone that could guide me in the right way of trading. The top traders sign a confidentially agreement not to disclose their trading strategies to anyone. No one was going to help me plan my life—I had to do it myself—so I decided to learn how to trade from other sources.

I started searching the internet for online training courses on how to trade in the Forex market. Unfortunately, most of the online training was either outdated and taught by people who had little to no experience in the Forex and commodity markets, or from brokers who want you to open an account and teach you incorrect strategies so you lose your money, and they make a good return out of you. But I didn't know about that when I started trading the market. I had so many ups and downs on my trading performance, I even burned a couple of accounts, until I realized that what I had learned so far about trading was totally wrong. I didn't learn about risk management, trade position sizing, or how to control my emotions (now they call it the "psychology of trading") until I lost a large amount of money, which made me sick for months. At that moment, I thought that trading was simply a gambling business and I should stay away from trading in the financial market. I stopped trading for a couple of years after acquiring large amount of debt.

I felt as if my planning had failed. However, I then realised I just didn't have the right information when I created my plan. You have to have a plan, but you also need to be armed with correct information before you make your plan. My plan to learn trading on my own to help diversify my income was a good plan, but my steps to execute it were all wrong. If your plans fail, go back to the steps and re-evaluate. I realised I had simply gone to the wrong sources—online courses. At that moment, I decided to seek out better sources to help me do it correctly. I found the books *Reminiscence of a Stock Operator: Story of Jesse Livermore*, written by Edwin Lefèvre, and *Trading in the Zone* by Mark Douglas. These two books in particular made me aware that trading can be treated as a business rather than gambling. I learned that I should not expect to become rich from trading overnight, but I can expect consistent results which create a weekly and monthly income. Now, I had better steps to execute my plan: learn from the right sources (real traders who are on the market), start slower, and work on earning consistent results rather than large amounts right away.

Even with the right plan, I encountered some obstacles. When I started searching for the best traders in the market, I found that they were all living outside my country. This meant I would have to pay extra for travel and hotel expenses on top of the coaching and mentoring fees. I would also have to take additional time off work. But my father had taught me when I was a child that I should not think about the cost when it comes to learning new things, since the value I will gain will be worth it. So, since I had to do these things in order to succeed in the market as a professional trader, I had to make those sacrifices. I joined traders' trading floors; travelled to Singapore, London, and New York to learn from the top traders in the market; and opened an account to start trading again. All this increased my confidence in trading in the market again, as I saw these professional traders make their income from trading. Just like that Chinese proverb advises, I took the time to grow my confidence before trading again.

Yes, I had initially failed. But remember, achievers never fail; they simply learn and grow. I grew from those initial failures, and I did something with that information. Since I wished I had learned correct trading strategies before I lost my initial investments in the market, I started teaching new traders to become successful in the market through my online membership site and my one-on-one coaching. You can check those out or wait for my next book, in which I teach my trading secrets.

Please note that investments can be risky if you don't know what you are doing, so I really advise that you proceed with real caution and consult your advisor before investing in any business venture.

Coaching Exercise: The Financial Goal-Achieving Process

Write down your top three one-year goals:

1.
2.
3.

By _____, my net worth will be _____.

By _____, I will have earned _____for my products/services.

These are the beliefs and declarations I am now accepting as true for me:

The main reasons why I must and will achieve this goal:

These are the new beliefs and habits that I must create now to achieve my goals for financial success:

After following the process and writing these goals, the most important thing is to take action. Knowing these goals is good, but without taking actions towards your goals, it is not valuable. It is just a goal written on a piece of paper without any benefit. So now you have to create action steps. First, you may want to read the next chapter, where I teach you how to create a business before making your action steps.

This is how I will achieve my goals:

By _____ (e.g., June 2017), I will start taking these actions:

1. (e.g., Read books about financial trading)

2. (e.g., Network with business-minded people)

3. (e.g., Start putting my business online)

4.

5.

6.

7.

Chapter Summary

I hope you enjoyed reading this chapter and learned from my experiences.

- Make a goal to become financially free within a realistic time frame.
- If your plan goes awry, revisit your steps and see if you need to change your action steps to better help you fulfil your goals.

STEPS TO CREATE AND SYSTEMIZE YOUR BUSINESS

5

In this chapter, I will give you a few tips on how you can create your own business and systemize it. I will also discuss owning a business while you are still working your current job, and then you can decide whether you want to stay in a job that you like while running your business or leave your job to focus on your business.

SECTION 1: WHY YOU MIGHT WANT TO START YOUR OWN BUSINESS

Having a business can be a way to express who you are through your products or services. It can be a place to grow and have fun, and it can provide peace of mind and increased certainty. Creating your own business can ensure you have more than enough income to live the lifestyle that you want, more than enough time and money to give back to your community and/or charities, and the security of your future and possibly your legacy.

This is exactly what I did when I reached my own financial freedom through my businesses and through trading in the market. I contributed to other people's self-development and volunteered my time to mentor young generations through youth-development communities in my country. In addition, I donate a percentage of my income to charities such as Doctors without Borders, UAE. This has motivated me and given me meaning and purpose. Thus, I work hard on growing my business while continuing my career as a senior corporate banker.

Section 2: How to Create a Business

As I mentioned, there was a period in my life when I was in deep debt and depressed. Then I heard this quote from Jim Rohn while listening to one of his DVD recordings: "If you work hard on your job, you will make a living, but if you work hard on yourself, you will make a fortune." I took that advice by the letter. I spent hours and hours after I got home from work and hours during the weekend working on myself. I sacrificed my holidays to attend seminars abroad on various subjects. I did whatever it took to develop myself, and I had coaches holding me accountable for reaching my goals in a shorter period. After all this, I was ready to create my own business.

Questions to Ask to Decide What Business to Start

Most successful businesses are designed around an ability to solve a problem, provide services that people need, or create an opportunity. If you are planning to set up a business, first ask yourself is what gifts, skills, and experience you have that can help other people.

Second, ask yourself how much extra income you would love to earn a month and what you would do with it.

Be very clear on what business you want to set up.

You have to remember that your first business should not make you overwhelmed just by thinking about it. It should at least be derived from something you know, something you have experienced, and something you know others will benefit from.

How to Set up Your Business

If you are new or have no idea how to set up your own business, the best first step is to hire a business coach who is already running a business to guide you on how to run yours. He or she will guide you through strategic tactics and tools that can help you establish and operate your business successfully.

Along with getting a coach, I have provided a step-by-step process to set up your business. This is the exact process I used to establish my first business. As I mentioned earlier, setting up a business normally takes between six months and one year to reach its full capability and capacity to perform.

Step 1: Establish Positivity and a Plan (Time: One Week)

Once you got the idea for your ideal business, write it down. Centre your thoughts and positive feelings on your business. Don't give in to negative thoughts when thinking of obstacles.

Keep this formula in mind:

Thoughts ➡ Feelings ➡ Action = Results

Every day, our mind receives a huge amount of thoughts. We either accept them or reject them based on our feelings. If we have deep positive feelings about a thought, we normally tend to take action, and if we take the proper action, it will provide good results. So make sure you think positively about your ability to start a business.

The second part of this step is to start working on the business plan. It should not take more than one week to work on it and write all the specific details. You may find that you don't have all the details about this kind of business, so I suggest you ask, search online and offline, and look for others who have already established this kind of business.

You must first create a plan before you take action. Without a business plan, it is easy to get trapped in the process until you realise that you are not going in the right direction to establish your business. And engineer who wants to build a house, he or she will draw it and design it on paper before going ahead and executing the project. Likewise, you must do the same.

THE MAIN ADVANTAGES OF HAVING A BUSINESS AND MARKETING PLAN:

1. It will help you determine if this is the right fit for you and your vision. Creating a plan will help you think about all the possibilities and anticipate any potential difficulties or losses at the beginning of the project.
2. It is a tool to persuade bankers, lenders, and investors who are going to be interested in your business that their money will be safe with you and you are in control of the business.

3. The business plan will help you calculate the risk and anticipated profit and will ensure future sustainability.

The main business plan outlines include the following:

- Company business objective
- Business module description
- Company description
- Goals and objectives
- Critical success factors
- Products and services
- Description of products and services and why they are unique
- Target market
- Target clients
- Competition/or creative idea (I do not like to mention competition because I really see opportunities in collaboration with others, and the market is open for everyone)
- Industry analysis
- History/current status
- Future sustainability

This is just an outline of the main points of the business plan. If you would like to have full instructions on how to write your own business and marketing plan, drop me an email at maitha@wayofachievers.com with the subject line "Business & Marketing Plan" so I can send it to you as thank you gift for purchasing this book.

Step 2: Create a Timeline for Yourself

I suggest you create an implementation plan: a timeline of when you will get everything done. List all the steps you need to take to create your business and determine when you want to start it and complete it. This is just an example table. You will most likely have more action steps, including the ones needed to create an online presence, but this is just an example of how you can set up a timeline for yourself.

Action item	Start date	Completion date
Get business license		
Contact lenders/investor		
Contract with supplier		
Buy machinery on discount or rent it for the first three months		
Create advertising plan		
Hire staff		
Grand opening		

Step 3: Search the Legality of Your Business and Select a Name for Your Business (One Week)

It is really worth the time to visit your municipality's chamber of commerce or economic development authority to get guidance on the business you are going to establish. The customer service desk will be able to guide you on the best way to set up this kind of business: what legal forms you need; how to determine if it is going to be a sole proprietorship, partnership, limited liability company, or corporation.

Once the authority approved your business model, they will ask you if you have selected a name for your business. You should think about this up front, because a business name can be a strong branding tool for your product and the way you serve others. It is also worthwhile to see if the online domain for the name that you have selected is available.

If the name is available, you can register it right away and get it trademarked. In my country, once you register the name, it will be valid for three months; after that period, you either register the company or renew the validity of the trade name for a further period.

Step 4: Set up an Online Version of Your Business (Three to Four Weeks)

Some businesses may be solely online, and that is fine. But if your business is offline, still try to take advantage of creating an online presence.

This is one of the best tools available in this century. Take advantage of it. Not only do you want a webpage, but you should also create social networks to reach a bigger online audience. You can create a simple landing page with a short video detailing what you offer. In addition, think of hiring a good online marketer who can support you in advertising your products or services to reach a wider audience. For this, I outsource most of my online tasks, like hiring a website developer, marketer, and social network marketer. But you have to ensure that you start with a low budget and deal with someone who will provide you with weekly reports of what they have done.

Step 5: Contact Potential Lenders and Investors

If your business project requires a large amount of funding, then it is better to raise funds. I know banks will not fund a start-up project, so the best way is either to find investors or business partners or to raise funds by targeting your potential clients via giving them huge offers like discounts on the service or products or a membership if they pay in advance for future delivery of your products or services.

If your business is on a large scale, like a manufacturing company, contact companies who will be willing to buy your products and sign agreements with them. Keep your cost low at the start.

Step 6: Location and Skilled Staff

If location is important for your business, then start searching for an ideal location. Do you want it in a mall, on a big city thoroughfare, or simply in an office near your home? Location plays a major part when setting up your business. I have seen many businesses fail within months of establishment not because of their products and services that they offer but because of their business location. It is also worth the time to check with the economic department for their advice on the location.

This is also a good time to start thinking about the skill sets needed for staff. What do you need to help you run your business—a finance manager, an accountant, a general manager, etc.—and what skills do they need?

Remember, you are a business owner, and you need to hire the right skilled employees to work on your business while you are managing it overall. This then takes is to the next level, which is systemizing your business.

SECTION 3: SYSTEMIZE YOUR BUSINESS

When I started creating my businesses, one of the secrets that I learned is systemization; this word is the basis of establishing a business. Once you systemize, you let your business work for you. With systemization, you will be the person who owns the business and not the person required to run the day-to-day operations. You will have more freedom and more choices. When I learned the secret of systemization, I immediately systemized my first business and then worked on creating other businesses and systemizing them as soon as they were established.

I see systemization as a necessary business tool that will allow you to streamline your business function and produce consistent and predictable outcomes. With systemization, you will need to work on entire guideline rules and policies that your team will follow to complete the production cycle even when you are not around. This will allow the company to run smoothly and productively, generating consistent income.

The business will become more profitable if you can leverage your time to work on strategies and then delegate the tasks to your implementation team rather than doing it yourself.

When systemizing your business, you need to do the following:

- Outsource tasks with low expected costs. These days, with all the technologies available to us, from internet access to cell phone to apps, it is easy to find others and outsource.
- Understand or recognise the workflow of your business, observe what the process will look like all the way to completion, and test out your process idea and see how it can work best.
- Streamline the process through using technology.

- Borrow others' ideas. If the business you want to set up already exists, there is no harm in visiting similar businesses to see how they operate and then use some of their ideas to systemize yours.
- Create clearer job descriptions with roles and responsibilities that each staff member will follow.
- Buy a system or software that your staff can work on to produce results if your company needs this.
- Set up the organisation structure, staff manual, and rewards policy to encourage high achievement.
- Ensure that you have put all aspects of your business on autopilot and clearly managed it from the start.
- Ask your company manager to provide you with weekly reports on performance, profit generated, and any issue or suggestion to improve things.

Starting and running a business can be overwhelming. Things like administration work, accounting, services, production, operations, marketing, and so on are so time-consuming when you are first trying to get your business out there, so it is best to learn how to systemize from day one to prevent you from having to take care of all those things.

Section 4: How to Find the Right Business Partner

If you're looking for a partner, it is important to find the right one. From my experience, there are a few things you need to check before entering into a business with a partner. Whether this is your first time creating a business or you already have multiple successful businesses, you need to check out any potential partners. When you are successful, many people will want to do business with you so they can succeed too, so make sure to check everyone carefully.

You should check all potential candidates' business backgrounds and their relationships with people. Have they created any kind of business before, and were those businesses successful? Do they have the skills to be a partner, or are they better suited to just work for you as a hired employee?

The big advice I can give here is not to hire a teacher who only talks theoretically and does not actually have a business. If they are a teacher and a businessperson, it is fine. But do not get caught in the trap of thinking all teachers of business are good at business.

SECTION 5: HOW TO MANAGE HAVING A CAREER AND RUNNING A COUPLE OF BUSINESSES

You might have heard of people who became financially successful by creating their own business and left their career to enjoy their time and financial freedom. This might be true for some people, but not for all. Some kept their job along with owning their own business.

You see when you reach your own financial freedom, you will start looking at things from a different perspective, especially when you are in a career that you love and you view your contribution as important. This is the case for me. Despite creating my own businesses and money-making vehicles, I still see that I need to contribute to others in my developing country, to share my experience with youth, and to help people create successful lives on their own terms. It gives me great pleasure to see a person whom I coached and mentored become successful. And it gives me an opportunity to practice my leadership skills.

The key is when you love what you do, it becomes a hobby, not a job, and you will sacrifice your time and effort to continue it. When there is no financial stress, contributing and making decisions comes naturally and powerfully.

You don't need to work at your job after creating a successful business unless you want to. But if you want to, you can.

This might sound too good to be true and hard to believe, or it might sound like hard work, but in reality, it is not. It is hard work at the start, but soon it becomes easy to manage. The initial process can take at least six months to one year, based on the business that you are setting up. So expect some long hours and hard work during the time when you are just starting your business.

When I started working on setting up each of my businesses, it took a lot of time and many sacrifices. I couldn't spend time with my family and friends during the weekend. It was even harder for me because I didn't have the ability to set my business up online in a few days like you can do now. While technology does make it easier, you must be aware that it will be a lot of hard work at first.

With this century of improved technologies and immediate gratification, we want what we want now and just the way we want it. We want overnight growth, instant mastery, and flawless performance on the first try. But that is not the way success is achieved. All successful people had to first put in the hard work, employing patience and perseverance to achieve fulfilment. Your pace is irrelevant to perseverance; it does not matter how slowly you go, as long as you don't stop.

Most successful people started their business as a side business while they were still working at their job.

This technique of setting up a business while you still working on a job requires the following:

- keeping an open mind to new ideas
- dedicating time each day (at least two to three hours in the evening) to work on and plan this new business
- having a business coach who is already successful, who will help them minimise their times and efforts in creating the business and provides better ideas on how to create it in a way that it will be profitable
- systemizing, systemizing, and systemizing

Once this business becomes successful and starts generating consistent income, the next step is to either duplicate that business like an automated machine or create another kind of business. This process will excite you more when you know exactly how to systemize and start duplicating the income.

COACHING TIP: ALWAYS AVOID CONFLICTS OF INTEREST

If you want to continue having your job as well as running your business, ensure that there is no conflict of interest between what you do in your career and the way you run your business. In my senior corporate banking career job, it is mandatory that we sign and adhere to a conflict-of-interest policy, which clearly states that we not create an environment whereby we exchange businesses or clients from our job in the organisation for our own personal advantage or for our business. Therefore, you must ensure you do not cross the line at your job and you keep your business and job separate.

CHAPTER SUMMARY

This chapter covered some tips on how to start a business and how to maintain both your job and your business.

- Create a business plan.
- Set a clear timeline on when you will get certain tasks done.
- Build an online presence.
- Hire a business coach.
- Outsource many of the tasks.
- Borrow others' ideas.
- Create clear job descriptions and hire skilled employees.
- Find the best location.
- Do not hire a teacher to be your business partner.
- Understand that it takes hard work and effort in the beginning; you must be focused and dedicated.

GO FORWARD DESPITE ALL OBSTACLES

6

In this chapter, I will illustrate why it is so important to keep going and keep working on yourself despite failures and obstacles. I will give you some examples from my own life, showing how I overcame various obstacles and challenges and the secrets behind what kept me going forward.

So, let's dive in together!

SECTION 1: LEARNING TO GO FORWARD AND MOVE PAST OBSTACLES

I grew up in a culture where girls were not allowed to do certain things. My culture believed this protects girls. Growing up, my mom would tell me I couldn't do certain things: I couldn't ride my bike outside with the boys, and I couldn't play football with my cousin. I didn't like it, and I wanted to prove to my mother that I wasn't like the other girls and she could trust me. This became a motivating factor for me. Whenever I faced adversity or failure on my journey to success, I would remember my mother, and I worked hard to prove I could do it. Find what will motivate you. This is different for everybody.

When I had my first job, I told my mother that one day I would establish a successful business and create an income-generating machine which would lead me to financial freedom, but she didn't believe me. She told me I wouldn't succeed because I was not a man, and this kind of business needed a man to run it, not someone like me.

I know that my mother loves me deeply, and she responded that way because she cared and wanted to protect me from failure. But guess what. I did fail, when forming a couple of companies in 2002, which at that time made me feel as though my mother was right.

Then I heard Jim Rohn in one of his lectures say, *"Don't wish it was easier. Wish you were better."* These words motivated me and drove me to work hard and succeed. I knew that I had to keep trying. If I stopped right then, I would have been a failure. Instead, I kept working on myself, on my belief, and on my own businesses until I found success.

This, of course, was not easy, and it didn't happen to me overnight. All achievers "fail" more than they succeed. However, they focus on what they learned, and thus they never really truly fail.

I realized then I could overcome the obstacles, but I had to work hard, believe, and be willing to take risks. I believe that a person who does not take risks, whether risking one's finances or one's time, will not succeed and can't be called an achiever. If you don't try, you will not fail, but if you don't fail, you will not succeed. People who don't take the time to try new things and experience failures will not succeed.

Don't get me wrong: I know that people can learn from other people's failures, so they don't experience the same failure; this is one of the purposes for this book— is for you to learn from my experience. Learning from other people's mistakes is always beneficial. However, learning from your own obstacles and challenges provides the best experience.

The key is not to let the obstacles stop you from achieving.

Section 2: Obstacles You May Face

You can overcome these obstacles. Always believe in yourself and reach for and sustain your potential. Get back up stronger even when you fail miserably; this is the only way to succeed. Jim Rohn said it best: *"Don't wish it was easier. Wish you were better. Don't wish for less problems. Wish for more skills. Don't wish for less challenge. Wish for more wisdom."*

Most of us have big goals, big dreams in life that haven't yet been achieved. Why? I think there are few factors that keep us from achieving these goals.

Obstacle #1: Fear

At the top of the list is fear: the fear of failure and the fear of success. While you often recognize your fear of failure, you do not always realize you fear your own success, which contributes more to your inability to achieve.

Obstacle #2: Lack of Clarity

Often, the reason we do not achieve our goals is that we do not know exactly what we want. My coach brought this to my attention. He asked me, "What do you really want?" I would always respond with what I didn't want: I didn't want to continue working for this bank and move into new one. I didn't want to be fat anymore. I didn't want to have large debts... I didn't... I didn't. My coach then told me, "If you continue focusing on what you don't want, you for sure will get more of it." Your subconscious mind does not know the difference between what you really want and what you don't want. Thus, if you continue thinking about being fat or having large debts, you will continue to have that and a lot more. You need to think differently. You need to focus on what you do really want.

Along with knowing exactly what you want, you must have a specific goal, which means you should not say, for example, "I want to lose weight." That is not enough. You should provide specific details, for example, I want to lose 20 kg in four months. Then, once you have a specific goal, follow the effortless formula outlined in chapter 3.

Remember, you need specific action steps with all the details. You could say you will allocate time to go to the gym five days a week, eat healthy food, or follow a specific diet. However, you want to determine all the details of that action step. So, for example, with the action step of going to the gym, outline what you will do at the gym and how many calories you will burn each session. With the action step of eating healthy, determine what that specifically looks like and means.

Obstacle #3: Thinking It Is Too Late

I deeply love horses. Growing up, I saw my brother ride and take care of his own horse. I wanted to learn horse riding for long time, but I didn't get a chance to do that until three years into my first working career. I thought that it might be too late, as I had already turned 22, but now I believe it is never too late to try something new, whether we are at the beginning of our lives or in its later stages.

Instead of thinking it was too late, I took action and visited the equestrian club in my city to seek this goal. Because I had definite goals of learning horse riding and becoming good at it in six months, I took the time to plan and set small action steps, such as reading books that teach the techniques of riding horses, watching online videos, and working with a personal trainer.

Obstacle #4: Finances

I still remember a time when I wanted to learn accounting through distance learning. At that time, I was just starting my first job, and my salary was insufficient to pay for the training course. However, the desire to learn to be good in accounting and the vision of having this degree overrode my anxiety over not having the money. With this, I managed to find a way to fund this education. It was painful at first, as I sacrificed time with my peers because I didn't have money to go with them, but the money went towards a larger value when I kept the big picture in mind.

Obstacle #5: Negative People

Never share your ultimate vision in public or with negative surroundings. Do not share in detail what you are planning to do or who you are going to involve in the process. Negative people will always try to pull you down, and you might get distracted into following their advice rather than pursuing what you want.

Obstacle #6: Thinking It Is Too Big to Achieve

A goal may seem too big to achieve, but if you break it up into smaller goals and plan wisely, you can do it.

I remember when I was in elementary school, my younger sister, who was in fifth grade at that time, came to me crying. I asked her why she was crying, and she said that the girls who were the first three in her class were not willing to be friends with her because she was twenty-seventh in a class of thirty-two, and they only become friends with clever girls. I encouraged her and told her she could become one of the top in the class. She lamented that it was impossible because she was not clever. I replied, "Yes, you can do it. Nothing is impossible. You can achieve this goal, maybe not this year but next year." I told her I would help her plan and work towards it.

I worked with her during the summer holiday, and I showed her how to plan her study by setting small weekly goals. In the first semester of the next year, she was fourth in the class, which surprised everyone. Those top three in the class came to her and wanted to be her friends. Afterwards, she continued following the same plan and always stood first or second in her class, until she graduated high school in the 93.4 percentile.

All this was achieved with simple goals and weekly planning.

Section 3: Overcoming My Greatest Obstacle

The only time you fail is when you fall down and stay down.
—Stephen Richards, *Cosmic Ordering: You Can Be Successful*

I have had to overcome many obstacles. However, I remember when I faced the hardest one: losing my initial investments when I started trading. From the perspective of any outsiders and my family, I looked fine. I had a good-paying job, I drove a nice car, and I was continuing my master degree education. But what they didn't realise was that I was trading in the financial market and losing big time. I hid in my room, so I rarely interacted with my family, as I didn't want to express and feel the pain that I was having back then and I didn't want them to know what I was doing. They thought that I was sleeping for long hours in my room. In fact, I was trading—actually, I was gambling—in the market. I had become addicted. I wanted to get back what I had invested, but this caused me to lose more and more, increasing my debt to $250,000 in 2004.

On top of that, I left my job, which was the only income for me back then, because someone promised me we would soon start our own brokerage company. That person didn't start the company, and I didn't work for one full year. I lost all my savings. I adopted an unhealthy lifestyle of eating unhealthy foods, and I became overweight to the point of obesity as I became an emotional eater. The doctor told me if I didn't take care of my health, I would have heart disease.

For a full year I was suffering, and I became so miserable until my mother finally discovered what was going on with me. Then I started looking for new job. By mid-2005, I started my new career. It took me years to recover financially and emotionally, but I did it. I came back from that much pain and loss.

My point here is that you have to overcome all obstacles, even ones that you inflict upon yourself. If you make bad decisions, if you take the wrong action steps, if you stop believing in yourself, you can pick yourself back up and fix it. There is no other way. If you don't work towards your goals and give up, you will settle for less than you truly are. So, hustle and keep working, and you will succeed with all your goals and desires.

COACHING TIP

After going through this chapter, you may still think that overcoming obstacles is not an easy task. In any area of your life, if you decide to make the decision to deal with and overcome any obstacle whether small or big, you will definitely overcome it. You must make that decision now: decide never to let obstacles stand in your way. I have seen people get over obstacles. Even when they struggle in the beginning, they do overcome them over time, once they decide to change their life. You must think positively, realise it is possible, and decide to overcome it.

COACHING EXERCISE: OVERCOMING NEGATIVE THOUGHTS ABOUT CREATING A BUSINESS

What are the negative thoughts you have about a new business opportunity, career experience, or investment?
(e.g., It is complicated. It takes more time and effort. It is hard work. It is Risky! Only rich people can invest in it. It needs more money for investments.)

What are some of the negative experiences that you had around creating your own business or having a better career and investments?
(e.g., I previously lost all my investments, I failed in my first business venture and got scared of changing my career to the one I always wanted.)

And what were your thoughts about them?
(e.g., It is hard to start over. It is better to spend the money and enjoy it now than putting it into investment.)

Write down all your personal experiences around handling money. (e.g., I lost $250K in the Forex market by using all the wrong tools. I was basically gambling, not trading. I spent more than I earned using credit cards and loans.)

If you were to take action despite these negative thoughts, what action would you take?
(e.g., I will always study and learn about the investments and make a plan before taking my decision. If someone tells me not to move to new career or business opportunity, I will always thank them for caring, and I will move on, because this is their experience and not mine.)

What new beliefs can you adopt right away to be financially successful?
(e.g., Invest wisely and smartly to create financial freedom that I desire. First invest, then compound, and later spend.)

I do not believe in taking the right decision, I take a decision and make it right.
—Muhammad Ali Jinnah

CHAPTER SUMMARY

This chapter motivated and encouraged you to overcome your obstacles.

- Decide now that you won't let obstacles stand in your way.
- Find what will motivate you.
- Be willing to take risks.
- Learn from your mistakes and failures.
- You can always overcome even the biggest of obstacles.
- Let go of your fears.
- Be clear on exactly what you want and how to get it.
- Realize that it is never too late.
- Be willing to pay for what is important and will be of great value to you.
- Avoid negative people.
- Realize that nothing is too big for you to achieve.

WHAT YOU DIDN'T LEARN IN SCHOOL

7

I am a believer in continual learning, not the kind of formal education that you get from schooling to qualify you for the career you want to pursue but continual self-development and learning that you don't find in formal school, topics like wealth creation, investment, business, financial trading, and risk management—even simple things like how to handle money.

This kind of learning you will only get from people who have experienced it: businesspeople, entrepreneurs who have established these businesses, and coaches. Of course, you will not get certificates from those trainings, but more importunately, you will have experience and self-development skills that you will use forever. I wish that I had this kind of learning before I started trading in local shares in 1999.

SECTION 1: LEARN SKILLS FOR YOURSELF FROM THE RIGHT SOURCE

You want to make sure you learn skills for yourself and you don't just take anyone's advice. When I first started trading, I took advice from a broker in the local market. The problem was that I didn't have any training in that market. I just took his word for it and invested. It wasn't necessarily that his advice was bad; it was just that I didn't have the training to execute it properly.

Other times, you will be given bad advice, and if you don't have the right training and skills, you won't recognise it.

When I first started Forex trading, I was buying foreign exchange options contracts through brokers in the Bahamas and Spain based purely on their analysis and recommendation. Although I made good profits at the beginning, even double what I had invested, I had no control over my investments or the decisions, as the broker was confirming and suggesting trades over the phone. I would always agree because I didn't know anything about the market and I trusted their trade placement. As I made more money, I started to agree and trust them even more. Sadly, I lost all my investments and profits in one night, when I agreed to invest my entire money in Japanese yen (JPY) after a long telephone conversation with the broker providing me a full study on the market. At first, I thought that it was from a professional trader who really knew what he was doing, as the sales pitch for this trade was highly convincing. Since this company had made me money, I trusted them. At that time, I didn't have anyone to consult with. I did have a gut feeling something might be off, but I didn't listen to my gut. They had gotten me to trust them, and I lost it all.

After a while the broker company called me again; even knowing that I had lost my investment on the JPY contracts, they tried to convince me to invest again, but in Great British Pounds (GBP) this time. I took the offer, and I invested an additional $18K on those contracts with complete hope that it will work out this time. However, hope alone doesn't get you anywhere. So this time, I decided I needed to be armed with my own knowledge. So, I also studied the reports that they gave me, and this time the contracts succeeded, and I doubled my investment. Once that happened, I withdrew all my invested money and my profits and closed my account with that broker.

I learned my lesson to not make decisions based solely on someone's recommendation; instead, I would get the proper training and know how to do things for myself. Acquiring the right learning or knowledge from a trusted source is very important. Learn from people who have done it and became successful at it.

SECTION 2: TRADING TIPS

While my next book goes into detail about trading secrets, I do want to give a few pointers. You need to seek out the best mentors and traders in the market.

Statistics show that 90 to 92 per cent of all rookie traders lose their money within one to twelve months of investments in the global market. While you may experience some loss initially, the amount of loss can be reduced if you take the time to learn and practice. I am always surprised that while professionals like doctors, lawyers, and engineers spend the time and money to learn and practice before they start applying for jobs, most traders aren't willing to spend the money and time to learn from professionals, and they just take risks and lose.

You must learn about risk management. It is a psychological game, and the promises that brokers provide to the public are so high that anyone can start making instant profits as soon as they invest. People go ahead and invest due to all this without realising that instant wins can easily lead to losing your investments.

So take the time to learn and spend money to learn from a professional.

SECTION 3: THE PURPOSE AND DESIRE FOR CONTINUAL LEARNING

In any industry, if you have definity of purpose and a desire to learn, you will succeed in that business. So take the time and learn the basics first before risking your real hard-earned money. While it might appear expensive and time-consuming to learn first, that initial investment will save you a lot of money and sleepless nights. Therefore, take the time to learn and study before going ahead, carefully learn each step, and be completely focused during the learning. Just like when you are planting a seed, it will take time to first build roots, and then it will show up on the surface.

I totally believe in continuing education, and I admire the people who invest their money and time to learn these special skills to improve themselves and seek personal growth in many areas of their lives. These days, when I want to learn something new, I always pay in advance and book for an exclusive offer; this ensures I don't change my mind or come up with an excuse to skip the course. I will do whatever it takes to learn as much as possible.

In 2013, I attended Millionaire Mind Intensive, a signature program of T. Harv Eker, the author of *Speed Wealth* and *The Secret of Millionaire Mind*. It was a three-day program full of energy and fun. It was worth the investment to be a part of that program.

I was with my sister and my multimillionaire friend, who is in her late fifties, when we were introduced to a full program package called Quantum Leap. My friend and I were betting on the price of the course, as these types of programs are normally expensive and not everyone can afford to attend. This program consisted of five-course packages including business, personal growth, investments, and finance. Once we heard the price of the course, which was expensive on top of needing to pay for air travel and accommodations, we didn't second guess whether we should do it or not, nor did we worry about the time it would take. I knew that learning is priceless and worth the cost, even if I learned only one new thing. My friend didn't stop and say, "I am too old for this." She just quickly reserved her seat in the program. Even though she was already a multimillionaire, and some might have thought she wouldn't need this, she knows there is always a next level in life, and she wanted to continue to learn and grow to move to the next level. We could have seen the expense and location as challenges, but we didn't let them stand in our way.

I believe all successful people who achieve things in life and make a difference overcome and see the challenges as part of their process towards their goals, and they do not stop learning. They are successful because they always work towards moving from one level to the next and understand that learning is part of the process and necessary to achieve what they desire.

SECTION 4: FREE STUFF ISN'T AS VALUABLE

When it comes to learning, I am so surprised and disappointed by the people who are always looking for free stuff: downloading books or programs from the internet for free! People search for videos and lectures on the internet, thinking they can learn all they need to know that way. While some of the content is valuable, they are missing out on the full information. Over time, if they continue that way, they will not receive the value they are seeking in any area of their lives, and this will reflect badly on what they do.

When I was recovering from my debt, I saw one of the best mentors was providing one-on-one mentoring programs on how to trade professionally in the financial market for eighteen months. I wanted to be mentored by him, but the bad news was I didn't have the money. The program cost GBP15,000. However, I had to do whatever it took to take this program; I might not have been able to afford it financially, but I really couldn't have afforded to miss out on the value it offered, so I took a loan from the bank just to pay for this program. You can think whatever you want to think about it, but this has paid pay for itself in value. I thought of it as an investment in myself; I didn't think about the amount or how long it would take to me settle this loan. That course was the best thing I have ever done.

These days, I see that even when people do have the money, they are deterred by the cost and neglect the value that they would have received. They are always looking for free stuff. However, they do not hesitate to pay for their exotic vacation, which may cost more than the amount that they could pay for a training program, books, DVDs, and their own personal development.

Is the amount that you pay for any program or book bigger than you? Achievers do whatever it takes to grow themselves to be better than they are every day, every week, and every year. They are always growing, and that growth can only be achieved through learning. If you want to be a master in something, you must spend the time and money to learn it. Why do you think doctors spend years and years studying and sacrificing their leisure time and going into school debt? Because they know that once they achieve this, it will pay for their time, money, and efforts spent in the beginning of their career.

Don't just sit on the side-line, afraid of the cost. Is it that fear that holds you back? Is it that intangible value that you don't see right now that stops you from taking action? Or is it that you don't view investments in your personal growth as important as other investments?

Think for a moment. What holds you back? Do you want to take the path of achievers, or do you want to stay the way you are? I don't think you do; otherwise, you would not have grabbed this book and continued reading up till this page.

SECTION 5: TURN YOUR CAR INTO A LIBRARY OF LEARNING

I am always on the move and learning something new every day. I would feel unproductive if I didn't do something each day that helped me grow.

Over the last eight years or so, I gladly changed my habit of listening to the news on the radio. In my opinion, the world news does not add any value to most of us. In fact, it usually just increases our stress. I used to spend hours and hours driving to and from work every day, listening to news. In the morning, I would listen to news or a morning talk show where people call and complain over just about everything. When you are going to work and you hear all this complaining on the radio, imagine how that carries throughout your day. So one day, I decided that enough is enough; listening to news increased my stressed and didn't serve a purpose, so I started to search for different ways to give me that morning boost of positive motivation and good vibrations.

From that day, I decided to turn my car into a library full of learning DVDs, *Success* magazine's monthly reports, and audiobooks. So I now use my daily drive to listen to motivational, self-development, business, and leadership programs. Now I rarely listen to the radio, and when I do, I only listen to music.

This strategy provided me with great growth and made me realise that there is no limit to learning. So, turn off your radio and turn your car into a moving library to reduce stress and bring more productivity into your day.

SECTION 6: WHEN I REALIZED THAT I CAN ADD VALUE!

From all this continuing learning, I realised that I could give back to the community by volunteering as a mentor to support the youth community in my country, teaching them and coaching them to create their own lifestyle and wealth.

It is important to realise you are unique and nobody in the universe matches your same skill set. This means you can attract your own opportunities in life and people will come to you for your unique skills. When I first understood this, it opened my mind to many opportunities, as I started adding value to people and improving their lives.

I never envisioned this for myself until people started approaching me and asking me to teach them how I had started my businesses, or how I had done well trading, or how I had created other investments.

At first, I rejected the idea of being a teacher; it wasn't what I wanted. I had decided earlier on in my life that I did not want to be a teacher. However, I realised that training and mentoring others was different than being a teacher. I could be a trainer, a coach, and a mentor.

I am now a selected mentor at Emirates Foundation for Youth Development in Abu Dhabi, and at the Abdul Aziz Bin Humaid Leadership program in Ajman. This is one of the ways I contribute and give back to society: by creating new mindsets for success and achievement in my country.

In addition, I participate in the Earth Watch organisation to support the nature and wildlife environment. Each year, I take a part in Earth Watch environmental projects, both financially and physically. This is created by fulfilling the lifestyle that I always wanted with abundance.

If you would like me to coach you to live this kind of lifestyle or create one of your own by challenging yourself to move on to the next level of your life as an achiever, I will offer you a chance for two complimentary coaching sessions as a bonus to you for picking and reading this book this far. You can drop me an email at maitha@wayofachiever.com, and I will personally get in touch with you.

COACHING TIP

Well, what can I say? Congratulations on reaching this far in this journey. As you can see, it is vital to continue learning and having this mindset for life.

Let me ask you this: What is something you have wanted to learn but you have either been afraid to or haven't made time for?

You need to drop the fear and make time to learn it if you really want to create your own unique lifestyle and enjoy the life of achievers. Growth comes from learning new things. You need to continue to improve yourself, and that only comes from learning and allowing yourself to be coached by experts in their field. If you are looking to grow your business or you're trading in the financial market, then I will be glad to coach you in these arenas.

Don't think about the cost of a book or a program; instead, think about what it will cost you if you decide *not* to take that leap and learn. You must take responsibility for your own learning, because guess what—no one else will do it for you. Learning is a lifetime worth of growth and investments in yourself.

Continual learning is your key to unlimited success, progress, and happiness. Your mind will always keep you younger as you feed your mind with good stuff.

I hope I inspired you to take action through what I have illustrated in this chapter. As you allow me to coach you, I want you to look for things that you are passionate about and learn more about it.

Chapter Summary

- It is important to learn specialised skills for yourself and not just trust others' advice.
- You need to learn the skills so you can execute people's good advice properly.
- Seek out the best coaches and mentors for trading.
- Do not start trading in the market without first learning.
- Always take advantage of opportunities to learn more and move to the next level.
- If you just look for free stuff, you will miss out on important learnings.
- View learning as an investment in yourself and realise the cost is worth the value.
- Use the time you spend commuting in your car to listen to audio books and DVDs.
- Give back to your community by mentoring and teaching others.

TRANSFORMATION

8

I hope this book gave you value. By applying the strategies and the powerful tools that I mentioned in this book, you will be on your way to transforming into an achiever. Although you have been an achiever from the beginning, you may not have realized it or lived your life that way. It is time to believe and live the way of achievers. It is time for your game-changing moment.

GAME CHANGING MOVEMENTS—THE MOMENT THAT CHANGED MY LIFE (BREAKTHROUGH)

There was probably a time when you didn't believe in your capabilities and you just listened and followed others who might not have been is capable and experienced as you are, but they had the confidence to be doing what they were doing. If that is still you, then you need to realise you are made for more. When you do that, you will take the word "impossible" out of your vocabulary; you will become unstoppable and everything will be possible for you. This is when success becomes second nature, and you will have transformed to an achiever. People will start looking to you as an icon of success without knowing all the obstacles and all the challenges that you had to go through to achieve this success.

I discovered that I always used to let others lead me even if they weren't as experienced as me. I didn't have the confidence in myself to live up to my achieving potential. But then I had a breakthrough.

My breakthrough happened when I was attending a trading course led by an expert. I realized I already knew what he was teaching, and not only that, but I had developed my own trading strategies that seemed to get better results than the ones he was sharing. In that moment, I realised I needed to believe that I could be a leader too. When I made that decision and started teaching others how to trade in the market, amazing things happened to me.

Therefore, my advice to you is to stop doubting your greatness and start living an extraordinary life now. Start working on yourself and see what you need now to achieve the success that you want.

To achieve your own breakthrough follow these steps that I have mentioned throughout this book:

- Surround yourself with friends who will support you and a coach to encourage and guide you.
- Start doing the small things. Take small steps at a time and enjoy every moment of it as you progress. The key is to focus on one thing at a time until you complete it. Then you can move on to the next step or next goal as you progress forward.
- Become financially stress-free so you can have freedom of choice and flexibility.
- Start working on yourself today, as there is no tomorrow in the dictionary of achievers. Don't procrastinate, don't hesitate, and don't think that you are not good enough or capable enough.
- Don't waste your life living someone else's life or dream. Ask yourself, "What do I want to achieve in

this life?" and make it happen. Change jobs, build businesses, or go on adventures. You are capable of much more than you ever realised.

Things you need to master if you want to sustain your business or your brand in the marketplace:

- Focus, focus, and focus on one thing and one thing only until completion.
- Have simplified and systemized strategies based on your unique brand.
- Become consistent in your approach to the marketplace.
- Continuously add value to your customers.
- Expand your network to support your business at a low cost.
- Be passionate about your business.
- Have your own original experience in this field.
- Consistently innovate.
- Believe in yourself.
- Be persistent.

Your Way to Transformation

I have discussed how to transform throughout this book. As a final thought, I want to leave you with my best advice, some of which has already been mentioned but is worth repeating. Finally, I will share some new advice.

1. My best advice on achieving any goal

- Be clear on what you want, plan, and set daily and monthly tasks to stay focused.
- Be patient, persistent, and have discipline.

With this formula, you will achieve your goal in record time. When you don't achieve a goal at first, look at failure as an opportunity for learning and growth rather than a sign that you need to give up.

2. My best advice on how to be more committed to yourself

Make a point to challenge yourself regularly; this will help you not to get bored with your craft and see how well you progress. If your goal is to read one book every single month, then divide the book into small sections that you can read every day and commit to follow through as scheduled. By the end of the month, you will be amazed that you completed reading one book. Looking forward in one year, you will be proud of yourself for reading twelve books. This is called commitment.

3. Why hiring a coach is an essential step to ultimate business success

Successful people perform the best by building up their weaknesses rather than ignoring them. They build a foundation for success called accountability. Hiring a coach is essential. If you are truly eager to achieve your goals in record time, you should have someone who can hold you accountable, which is definitely the main mission of your coach. A coach creates a positive and nonjudgmental environment, and he or she will challenge you to achieve your goal and show you your true capabilities in achieving your ultimate business success.

4. Best advice to stick to your plan

I am well known for planning. The secret to all of my success is that I plan and have a clear vision. You must make a clear plan. However, it is okay to revise and change your plan if needed. You can review your plan until it suits you the best and meets your ultimate goals. However, once you have the best plan, you need to take action. A plan without action is a plan for failure.

5. Advice on motivating yourself as an entrepreneur

As an entrepreneur, I always create time for myself each day to be alone, away from all distractions. It makes me more productive. I always set time for myself daily, in a quiet place out in inspiring nature, to enjoy positive vibes away from the day-to-day routine of business. This helps me get motivated all the time; it also raises my standard and keeps me focused on what I want to do next. Next, I always set rewards for myself when I achieve even small goals.

6. Best advice on maintaining a healthy and a balanced life

My advice is to always respect boundaries between your work and life. Don't get trapped in distractions or things that are not productive for you. In addition, always avoid conflicts of interest between your career and your business; keep both at a distance from each other.

Jim Rohn said it best: "Don't mistake movement for achievement. It is easy to get faked out by being busy. The question is: Busy doing what?"

7. Entrepreneurial mistakes to avoid based on my experience

The biggest entrepreneurial mistakes to avoid from my own experience is saying "yes" to everything. If someone present a business idea to you, you should first do all your due diligence checks, like studying the market and seeing if the person who wants to be your partner is capable and trustworthy to do this business. It is okay to say no if the business proposal does not match your plans and your forward visions. The difference between successful and ultra-successful people is that ultra-successful people say no most of the time.

FINAL WORDS

Thank you for reading my book.

I hope you will help me spread these words to touch more people in to living the way of achievers and help them define the life that they desire by leaving an honest review for this book.